I0017523

The Evolution of Ai in Medicine

How Artificial Intelligence is Reshaping Drug Discovery, Patient Care, and the Future of Healthcare

Tommy jp. Hernandez

Table of content

Introduction

The Rise of AI in Drug Discovery

Artificial Intelligence (AI) is poised to revolutionize the field of drug discovery, offering unprecedented speed, efficiency, and accuracy in developing new medical treatments. Traditionally, the process of identifying and designing new drugs has been a laborious, costly, and time-consuming effort. It typically takes 10 to 15 years and over $2 billion to bring a new drug from concept to market. Furthermore, the success rate of clinical trials is notoriously low, with approximately 90% of drugs failing to make it through to approval. However, AI is changing the game by leveraging machine learning, deep learning, and other advanced technologies to expedite the process, reduce costs, and improve the odds of success. This transformative role is exemplified by companies like Insilico Medicine, where AI is not just a tool but a core driver of innovation in drug development.

The Need for Change in Drug Discovery

The traditional drug discovery process has long been fraught with challenges. It starts with the identification of a target, usually a protein or gene associated with a disease, followed by the design of molecules that can interact with that target to exert therapeutic effects. The path to identifying these molecules involves numerous stages, from laboratory experiments and animal testing to clinical trials. Each step is expensive, time-consuming, and fraught with risks, particularly the high failure rate in clinical trials. For example, in the United States, the average cost of developing a single drug is estimated at $2.6 billion, with the bulk of the expense incurred during the clinical trial phases. Furthermore, even successful drugs often take decades to reach the market due to regulatory hurdles and the complexity of trials.

These factors contribute to the slow pace of innovation in the pharmaceutical industry and hinder the rapid development of treatments for diseases, especially rare or complex conditions. For instance, diseases like idiopathic pulmonary fibrosis (IPF), which affects the lungs, have no known cure and limited treatment options. The slow pace of drug development for such diseases has prompted many experts to seek new approaches—approaches that could be far more effective in tackling the challenges of drug discovery. Enter AI, a technology that has already demonstrated its ability to speed up various industries and is now poised to do the same for medicine.

AI: The Game-Changer for Drug Discovery

AI in drug discovery leverages computational models to analyze massive datasets, predict molecular behavior, and optimize drug candidates more efficiently than traditional methods. Machine learning algorithms, deep learning networks, and other AI tools are used to identify drug targets, design molecules, and predict how these molecules will interact with biological systems. This new approach allows researchers to process and analyze vast amounts of data—such as genomic data, protein structures, and chemical properties—faster and more accurately than a human could.

One of the key advantages of AI in drug discovery is its ability to predict the efficacy of drug candidates before they ever enter the lab. By training AI models on data from existing drugs, biological systems, and disease mechanisms, these systems can learn to identify promising drug candidates in a fraction of the time it would take using traditional methods. This can significantly reduce the cost and time associated with the early stages of drug development, which are typically the most expensive and time-consuming.

AI can also help identify novel drug targets genes, proteins, or other biomolecules that may play a role in disease but were previously overlooked or difficult to study. AI algorithms can mine vast biological datasets, cross-referencing them with disease-specific information to discover potential new targets that could be addressed by therapeutic drugs. This ability to explore complex datasets and identify novel relationships between genes, proteins, and diseases is one of the reasons why AI is seen as a game-changer for drug discovery.

Insilico Medicine: A Pioneer in AI-Driven Drug Discovery

One of the standout companies leveraging AI for drug discovery is Insilico Medicine, a U.S.-based biotech startup co-founded by Alex Zhavoronkov in 2014. The company uses AI to discover new drugs for diseases that have traditionally been difficult to treat, such as cancer, fibrosis, and neurodegenerative diseases. Insilico Medicine has made significant strides in integrating AI into every stage of the drug discovery process, from target identification to drug design and optimization.

According to Dr. Zhavoronkov, Insilico Medicine is at the forefront of using AI to uncover useful molecules that may have a significant impact on human health. The company uses a combination of generative models and reinforcement learning to predict the properties of drug candidates and optimize them for efficacy and safety. Insilico Medicine's proprietary AI systems are capable of generating millions of new molecular structures, which are then tested and validated through laboratory experiments.

A breakthrough example of this is Insilico Medicine's work on idiopathic pulmonary fibrosis (IPF), a rare and progressive lung disease. In collaboration with other researchers, the company developed a novel drug candidate using its AI-powered systems. The drug was designed to inhibit a specific protein that plays a role in the progression of IPF, and early-stage clinical trials have shown impressive results. This drug represents a new wave of therapeutics that were not only discovered but also optimized using AI.

Dr. Zhavoronkov's vision for the future of drug discovery is one where AI plays a central role in the entire process. His belief is that AI can drastically reduce the time and cost of developing drugs while increasing the likelihood of success in clinical trials. While AI may never fully replace human researchers, it will act as an invaluable tool that accelerates discovery and augments human expertise.

AI and the Great Drug Race

The idea of AI revolutionizing drug discovery has captured the attention of the pharmaceutical industry at large. In fact, AI is now at the center of what has been dubbed the "great AI drug race." This race involves a growing number of biotech startups and established pharmaceutical companies leveraging AI to identify new drug candidates and develop innovative treatments for a wide range of diseases.

Among the new players in this field is Alphabet, the parent company of Google, which launched a UK-based AI drug discovery company called Isomorphic Labs in 2021. This initiative, led by CEO Demis Hassabis, is built on the success of the AI model that won Hassabis and his team the Nobel Prize in Chemistry in 2023. This AI model, which is capable of predicting molecular behavior, is expected to have significant implications for drug design and discovery. Alphabet's entry into the AI drug discovery space further validates the enormous potential of AI in transforming medicine.

However, Insilico Medicine is not alone in its quest to use AI for drug discovery. Other companies, such as Recursion Pharmaceuticals, are also leveraging AI to accelerate drug development. Recursion focuses on using AI to generate vast amounts of biological data, which it then uses to train its models to uncover new disease targets and potential drug candidates. This approach has already led to the development of a molecule that targets lymphoma and solid tumors, which is currently undergoing clinical trials.

These companies, along with many others, are racing to leverage AI to bring innovative new drugs to market faster, cheaper, and with a higher success rate. With billions of dollars being invested in AI-driven biotech startups, it is clear that AI is the future of drug discovery.

The Benefits of AI in Drug Discovery

The potential benefits of AI in drug discovery are vast and far-reaching. Some of the key advantages include:

1. **Speed and Efficiency**: AI can process vast amounts of data in a fraction of the time it would take humans to analyze manually. This speeds up the identification of drug targets, the design of drug candidates, and the testing of new molecules.

2. **Cost Reduction**: By reducing the time and labor involved in drug discovery, AI has the potential to

lower the cost of developing new drugs. This is especially important in the face of skyrocketing healthcare costs and the need for more affordable treatments.

3. **Increased Success Rate**: With AI's ability to predict molecular behavior and optimize drug candidates, the likelihood of success in clinical trials can be significantly increased. This not only saves time and money but also reduces the risks associated with drug development.

4. **Novel Drug Targets**: AI can help researchers identify new drug targets that may have been previously overlooked or too difficult to study. This opens up new possibilities for treating diseases that currently have limited therapeutic options.

5. **Personalized Medicine**: AI can be used to tailor treatments to individual patients based on their unique genetic makeup, improving the effectiveness of drugs and minimizing adverse effects.

Challenges and Limitations

Despite the immense promise, AI-driven drug discovery is not without its challenges. One of the key obstacles is the quality and availability of data. AI models rely heavily on large datasets, and the lack of high-quality data can lead to biases or inaccuracies in predictions. Furthermore, the complexity of human biology and disease mechanisms means that AI models are still far from perfect, and human expertise will remain essential in interpreting results and guiding decision-making.

Another challenge is the need for regulatory frameworks that can accommodate the rapid pace of AI-driven innovation. As AI becomes more integrated into drug discovery, regulators will need to establish new guidelines for assessing the safety and efficacy of AI-designed drugs.

AI is transforming the landscape of drug discovery, providing new opportunities to address some of the most pressing medical challenges. Companies like Insilico Medicine are at the forefront of this revolution, leveraging AI to design drugs faster, cheaper, and with a higher success rate than traditional methods. While there are challenges to overcome, the potential benefits of AI in drug discovery are enormous, and the future looks promising for patients in need of new treatments. As AI continues to evolve, it is likely that we will see even more groundbreaking advancements in medicine, ultimately improving the lives of millions of people worldwide.

Chapter 1: AI-Powered Drug Development: The New Frontier

In recent years, artificial intelligence (AI) has emerged as one of the most powerful tools in the life sciences sector, particularly in drug development. What was once a slow, labor-intensive, and highly expensive process is now being transformed by AI into something faster, more efficient, and capable of producing highly innovative solutions. The ability of AI to mine massive datasets, predict molecular behaviors, and optimize compounds has opened up new frontiers in biotechnology, enabling the development of novel treatments at an unprecedented pace. AI is quickly becoming the cornerstone of modern drug discovery, pushing pharmaceutical companies, biotech firms, and startups into a new era of medical breakthroughs.

This exploration of AI-powered drug development will delve into how AI is reshaping the drug discovery process, why the biotech industry is embracing it, the key players leading the charge, and the challenges that lie ahead.

The Traditional Drug Discovery Process.

The traditional drug discovery process has long been a laborious, time-consuming journey, typically taking between 10 and 15 years to bring a new drug from early-stage research to market. This lengthy timeline can be attributed to several factors, including the complex and often unpredictable nature of human biology, the intricacies of disease pathways, and the painstaking process of designing drugs to target those pathways. On top of that, drug development is incredibly expensive, with estimates suggesting that the total cost to bring a single drug to market is upwards of $2 billion.

The initial steps in drug discovery usually begin with identifying a disease target, such as a specific gene or protein implicated in a disease. Researchers spend years understanding how these targets function, how they are altered in disease, and which interventions can reverse or mitigate the harmful effects. Once a target is identified, the next step involves high-throughput screening, wherein thousands of compounds are tested to see if they can bind to the target and exhibit therapeutic effects. This stage is followed by optimizing drug candidates, conducting preclinical studies, and eventually entering clinical trials, where success rates are notoriously low. Approximately 90% of drugs that enter clinical trials fail, often due to unforeseen side effects or lack of efficacy.

Given these significant challenges, the pharmaceutical industry has sought ways to streamline and enhance the drug discovery process, and AI has emerged as the game-changer. AI models, particularly machine learning algorithms and deep learning networks, can process enormous datasets, identify patterns, predict the behavior of molecules, and even generate new drug candidates in a fraction of the time it would take using traditional methods. By harnessing AI, researchers can not only accelerate the development of new drugs but also make the process more cost-effective and reliable.

The Role of AI in Drug Discovery

At its core, AI in drug discovery refers to the application of machine learning, deep learning, and other AI technologies to enhance and accelerate various aspects of drug development. These technologies allow researchers to tap into vast amounts of biological, chemical, and clinical data to make predictions, uncover insights, and discover patterns that would be impossible for humans to find on their own. AI can optimize multiple stages of the drug discovery process, from target identification and molecule design to clinical trial optimization and personalized medicine.

1. Target Identification and Validation

The first and most crucial step in drug discovery is identifying and validating a disease target. Traditionally, this has been done through experimental research, using biological insights and human intuition to pinpoint the molecular targets most relevant to a disease. However, this method is time-consuming and prone to bias.

AI revolutionizes this process by mining massive biological datasets, such as genomic data, proteomics, and clinical information, to uncover hidden connections between diseases and molecular targets. By applying AI models that process and analyze these datasets, researchers can identify new druggable targets more quickly and accurately. For example, AI can be used to predict which genes or proteins are most likely to be involved in a disease's progression, even in cases where the underlying biology is not well understood. This ability to identify novel targets opens up new possibilities for drug development and can lead to treatments for diseases that previously had no targeted therapies.

2. Drug Design and Optimization

Once a target is identified, the next critical step is designing a drug that can interact with it effectively. Historically, this involved testing thousands of compounds manually in the lab to find one that binds to the target and produces the desired effect. This process is not only expensive but also time-consuming and inefficient.

AI-powered drug design, on the other hand, uses generative models to create novel compounds that are optimized for efficacy and safety. These models use large datasets to learn about the interactions between different molecules and predict how new compounds will behave. AI can generate millions of new molecular structures in a fraction of the time it would take using traditional methods, significantly speeding up the process of drug design.

Additionally, AI can help researchers identify the optimal molecular properties for a drug, such as its ability to bind to the target, its stability in the body, and its ability to cross the blood-brain barrier. By fine-tuning these properties early in the process, AI can help eliminate less promising candidates and focus resources on the most promising drug leads.

3. Predicting Drug Efficacy and Safety

AI can also predict how new drug candidates will behave in clinical trials. By analyzing historical clinical trial data and molecular properties, AI models can estimate the likelihood that a drug will be successful in treating a particular disease. These models can identify potential side effects, drug interactions, and other issues before a drug ever enters clinical trials, helping to reduce the risk of failure. Furthermore, AI can be used to simulate clinical trials, enabling researchers to test drug candidates virtually before conducting costly real-world experiments.

4. Personalized Medicine

One of the most exciting prospects of AI-powered drug development is the ability to create personalized treatments tailored to an individual's genetic makeup, lifestyle, and environment. By analyzing genomic and clinical data from diverse populations, AI can identify patterns in how different people respond to drugs. This allows for the development of treatments that are customized for specific genetic profiles, improving the effectiveness of treatments while minimizing adverse side effects.

AI-driven personalized medicine has the potential to revolutionize the treatment of complex diseases such as cancer, where a "one-size-fits-all" approach often does not work. By tailoring treatments to the individual's genetic profile, AI can ensure that patients receive the most effective therapies based on their unique biology.

The Growing Race to Leverage AI in Biotech

As AI continues to prove its potential in drug discovery, a growing number of biotech companies, large pharmaceutical firms, and startups are racing to capitalize on its capabilities. The biotech industry is undergoing a profound transformation as companies embrace AI to uncover new drug candidates, enhance research processes, and bring drugs to market faster.

A key example of this shift is Insilico Medicine, a biotech company founded by Alex Zhavoronkov in 2014. Insilico has been a pioneer in using AI to design and discover new drugs. The company's AI-driven platform uses generative models to design novel molecules for various diseases, including cancer, fibrosis, and neurodegenerative disorders. One of the company's most notable achievements is the development of a novel drug for idiopathic pulmonary fibrosis (IPF), a rare lung disease. Using its AI platform, Insilico Medicine was able to identify a novel drug target and design a molecule to address the disease, which has shown promising results in early clinical trials.

Another key player in the AI drug development race is Recursion Pharmaceuticals, which is leveraging AI to uncover hidden relationships in biological data. Recursion uses AI to analyze vast amounts of data from biological experiments, enabling the discovery of new drug targets and potential therapies. The company's AI platform has already yielded promising results, including the identification of a new drug for cancer that is currently in early-stage clinical trials.

Large pharmaceutical companies like Roche, Novartis, and Merck are also investing heavily in AI to speed up their drug discovery processes. These companies are partnering with AI-driven biotech firms or developing in-house AI capabilities to accelerate their research and improve the efficiency of their drug pipelines. AI is enabling these companies to identify drug targets, design molecules, and optimize clinical trial designs, all while reducing the time and costs associated with drug development.

Alphabet, the parent company of Google, entered the AI drug discovery space in 2021 by launching Isomorphic Labs, a UK-based biotech company focused on leveraging AI to develop new drugs. Isomorphic Labs aims to combine Google's deep expertise in machine learning with cutting-edge biology to create transformative drugs. The company's CEO, Demis Hassabis, who shared the Nobel Prize in Chemistry in 2023 for his work on AI models in biology, sees AI as the key to unlocking new treatments for diseases that currently have no cure.

Challenges and Considerations in AI-Powered Drug Development

Despite the enormous promise of AI in drug discovery, there are several challenges that remain to be addressed. One of the primary obstacles is the need for high-quality data. AI models are only as good as the data they are trained on, and in the life sciences, data can be sparse, noisy, and biased. High-quality biological data that accurately represents the complexity of diseases is crucial for training effective AI models.

Moreover, while AI can accelerate drug development, it does not eliminate the need for human expertise. AI models must be carefully designed, interpreted, and validated by scientists with deep knowledge of biology, chemistry, and pharmacology. AI should be seen as a tool to complement human expertise rather than replace it.

Finally, regulatory challenges remain. The use of AI in drug discovery raises questions about how to regulate AI-driven drug development, particularly with regard to safety and efficacy. Regulatory agencies such as the U.S. Food and Drug Administration (FDA) will need to establish guidelines for evaluating AI-designed drugs, ensuring that they meet the same rigorous standards as traditionally developed therapies.

AI-powered drug development is not just a passing trend; it is the future of medicine. By leveraging the power of AI, the biotech industry is accelerating the discovery of new treatments, reducing costs, and improving the success rate of clinical trials. Companies like Insilico Medicine, Recursion Pharmaceuticals, and Isomorphic Labs are leading the charge, with AI helping them to unlock new possibilities for addressing some of the most challenging diseases of our time. While challenges remain, the growing race to leverage AI in drug discovery signals a new frontier in biotechnology that promises to transform medicine for the better. As AI continues to evolve, the future of drug development will become faster, more personalized, and more effective, offering hope to patients around the world.

Chapter 2: The Role of Major Players: Insilico Medicine and Isomorphic Labs

In recent years, artificial intelligence (AI) has dramatically reshaped the landscape of drug discovery, enabling biotech and pharmaceutical companies to develop treatments faster, more cost-effectively, and with a higher probability of success. Among the leaders driving this transformation are Insilico Medicine, a pioneering biotech firm focused on AI-driven drug discovery, and Isomorphic Labs, a subsidiary of Alphabet (the parent company of Google), which is harnessing AI to accelerate the development of new therapeutics. Both companies are at the forefront of the AI revolution in healthcare, with their cutting-edge research yielding promising results in the fight against diseases that have long eluded effective treatment.

In this article, we will explore the groundbreaking contributions of Insilico Medicine and Isomorphic Labs, examining their innovative AI-powered platforms, their key discoveries, and the profound impact they are having on the future of medicine. Through these case studies, we will highlight how these two companies are leveraging AI to push the boundaries of drug discovery and offer new hope for patients suffering from a range of conditions.

Insilico Medicine: Revolutionizing Drug Discovery with AI

Overview of Insilico Medicine

Insilico Medicine was founded in 2014 by Dr. Alex Zhavoronkov, a scientist with a deep interest in AI and its potential to revolutionize the biotechnology and pharmaceutical industries. The company focuses on using artificial intelligence to design and discover new drugs, optimize existing therapies, and accelerate the drug development process. Insilico Medicine employs a range of AI technologies, including deep learning, generative adversarial networks (GANs), and reinforcement learning, to analyze biological data, predict the behavior of molecules, and generate new drug candidates.

The company is particularly well known for its work in creating generative AI models that can design novel drug molecules from scratch. Insilico Medicine's AI platform integrates multiple data sources, such as genomic, proteomic, and clinical trial data, to uncover hidden relationships and identify new therapeutic targets. This approach not only speeds up the drug discovery process but also reduces the failure rate of clinical trials, which has historically been a major barrier in bringing new drugs to market.

Key Discoveries and Achievements

One of Insilico Medicine's most notable achievements is its development of a novel drug for idiopathic pulmonary fibrosis (IPF), a progressive and deadly lung disease with no known cause or cure. The drug was discovered using the company's AI-driven drug discovery platform, which analyzed large amounts of biological and clinical data to identify a potential therapeutic target. The molecule designed by Insilico Medicine's AI was tested in preclinical models and showed promising results. This was a groundbreaking achievement because IPF had long been considered an intractable disease, and no effective treatment options had been found.

The development of the IPF drug marked a major milestone for Insilico Medicine. The company's AI system was able to design a molecule that effectively targeted a protein called TNIK (TRAF2 and NCK-interacting kinase), which had never been targeted before for IPF. The fact that Insilico Medicine's AI was able to pinpoint this target and design an effective molecule in a fraction of the time it would take using traditional drug discovery methods is a testament to the power of AI in transforming the drug development process.

In addition to the IPF drug, Insilico Medicine has successfully used AI to design molecules for a variety of other diseases, including cancer, fibrosis, and neurodegenerative conditions like Alzheimer's and Parkinson's. The company has built an extensive pipeline of AI-discovered molecules, with several currently in clinical trials. These advancements underscore the potential of AI to tackle some of the most complex and challenging diseases in modern medicine.

The AI Platform: How It Works

Insilico Medicine's AI platform is built on a combination of several advanced AI techniques, including deep learning, generative models, and reinforcement learning. At the heart of the platform is the company's proprietary generative chemistry model, which uses GANs to design novel drug-like molecules. Generative AI models are trained on large datasets of chemical structures and biological data, allowing the AI to learn how different molecular properties relate to therapeutic effects. This enables the platform to generate entirely new molecular structures that are optimized for specific disease targets.

One of the key advantages of Insilico Medicine's AI-driven approach is speed. Traditionally, drug discovery involves manually testing thousands of compounds in the laboratory, which can take years. Insilico Medicine's platform can generate millions of potential drug candidates in a matter of hours, dramatically reducing the time and cost associated with the early stages of drug development. Additionally, the AI platform helps prioritize the most promising candidates, allowing researchers to focus on the most likely therapies and avoid wasting time on compounds with little potential.

Beyond drug design, Insilico Medicine's platform also plays a role in optimizing clinical trial designs. The company uses AI to predict the likelihood of success for different drug candidates in clinical trials, taking into account factors such as patient demographics, molecular properties, and historical clinical data. This enables the company to make data-driven decisions about which compounds to advance and how to optimize trial designs for maximum efficacy.

Isomorphic Labs: Alphabet's Venture into AI Drug Discovery

Overview of Isomorphic Labs

Isomorphic Labs is a relatively new player in the biotech field, having been launched in late 2021 by Alphabet, the parent company of Google. Isomorphic Labs aims to revolutionize drug discovery by combining Alphabet's expertise in artificial intelligence with cutting-edge biology to create a new generation of therapeutics. The company's focus is on using AI to accelerate the development of drugs, particularly for diseases with high unmet medical needs.

The formation of Isomorphic Labs was inspired by the success of DeepMind, another Alphabet subsidiary, which developed AlphaFold, an AI model that has had a transformative impact on the field of protein folding. AlphaFold's ability to predict the three-dimensional structure of proteins has accelerated our understanding of biology and paved the way for AI-driven drug discovery. Isomorphic Labs seeks to build on this success by using AI to model complex biological processes and identify new drug candidates more efficiently.

Key Achievements and Contributions

Isomorphic Labs is still in the early stages of its journey, but it has already made significant strides in applying AI to drug discovery. One of the company's most ambitious goals is to use AI to understand the complex molecular biology of diseases and identify drug targets that have not yet been explored. By applying deep learning techniques to vast datasets of biological information, Isomorphic Labs hopes to uncover novel therapeutic targets and design drugs that can address unmet medical needs.

A major milestone for Isomorphic Labs was the announcement of its partnership with major pharmaceutical companies and research institutions to accelerate the development of new therapeutics. The company's platform has the potential to streamline the entire drug discovery process, from target identification to drug design and optimization. As part of its long-term vision, Isomorphic Labs aims to integrate AI across all stages of the drug development pipeline, reducing the time and cost required to bring new treatments to market.

One of the key areas where Isomorphic Labs is making an impact is in the development of drugs for complex diseases like cancer, neurodegenerative disorders, and rare genetic conditions. The company's AI models can analyze large volumes of genomic, proteomic, and clinical data to identify biomarkers and genetic mutations that are relevant to these diseases. By targeting these specific molecular alterations, Isomorphic Labs hopes to develop precision therapies that are tailored to individual patients.

The AI Platform: How It Works

Isomorphic Labs uses a range of AI techniques to develop new drugs, including deep learning, reinforcement learning, and generative models. The company's platform leverages Alphabet's advanced computing infrastructure to process massive datasets and uncover new patterns in biological data. By training AI models on data from genomic sequencing, clinical trials, and other sources, Isomorphic Labs is able to predict which drug candidates are most likely to be effective in treating specific diseases.

One of the key differentiators of Isomorphic Labs' platform is its integration with AlphaFold, the groundbreaking AI model developed by DeepMind. AlphaFold has the ability to predict the three-dimensional structure of proteins with remarkable accuracy, which is crucial for understanding how drugs interact with biological targets. By combining the power of AlphaFold with other AI techniques, Isomorphic Labs can design drugs that are optimized for specific proteins or disease pathways.

Isomorphic Labs is also focusing on using AI to streamline clinical trials. Traditional clinical trials are time-consuming and expensive, and many drugs fail in later stages of testing due to unforeseen issues with efficacy or safety. Isomorphic Labs aims to reduce the risk of failure by using AI to simulate clinical trials and predict which drugs are most likely to succeed. This can help prioritize the most promising candidates and design trials that are more likely to yield positive results.

Conclusion: Transforming Drug Discovery with AI

Both Insilico Medicine and Isomorphic Labs are leading the charge in the use of AI to accelerate drug discovery and bring new treatments to market. Through their innovative AI-driven platforms, these companies are transforming the drug development process, making it faster, more cost-effective, and more precise.

Insilico Medicine has already made significant strides in the discovery of new drug candidates, including its groundbreaking work in idiopathic pulmonary fibrosis, while Isomorphic Labs is using AI to tackle some of the most complex diseases, leveraging Alphabet's computing power and deep learning expertise.

As AI continues to evolve and become more integrated into drug discovery, these companies will play a pivotal role in shaping the future of medicine. The potential of AI to unlock new treatments for diseases that have long been difficult to address offers new hope for patients around the world, and the groundbreaking work of Insilico Medicine and Isomorphic Labs is a testament to the transformative power of AI in healthcare.

Chapter 3: The Challenges of Traditional Drug Development

The development of new drugs has historically been a long, costly, and high-risk process, often taking over a decade to bring a new treatment to market. Despite incredible advances in science and technology, the pharmaceutical industry has struggled to find ways to significantly reduce the time, cost, and failure rates associated with drug development. However, with the advent of artificial intelligence (AI), a potential revolution in drug discovery and development is on the horizon. AI offers the promise of streamlining the development process, cutting down on the costs, and reducing the risk of failure. In this article, we will explore the traditional challenges of drug development and examine how AI could transform this complex and costly process.

The Traditional Drug Development Process.

The Phases of Drug Development

Traditional drug development typically follows a series of well-established phases: discovery, preclinical testing, clinical trials, and regulatory approval. Each phase is designed to ensure that new drugs are safe and effective before being made available to the public. Let's take a closer look at these stages:

1. **Discovery Phase**

   This initial stage involves identifying a potential therapeutic target, such as a gene, protein, or pathway that is involved in the disease being studied. Scientists may identify a target through laboratory research or by studying existing medical knowledge. After the target is identified, compounds that could potentially interact with the target are screened.

2. **Preclinical Testing**
   - After promising compounds are identified, they undergo preclinical testing. This

stage involves laboratory studies and tests on animals to assess the safety, toxicity, and efficacy of the compounds. The aim is to determine if the drug candidate has potential for human use.

3. **Clinical Trials**

   o If preclinical tests are successful, the drug candidate progresses to clinical trials. Clinical trials are typically divided into three phases (I, II, and III), each of which involves testing the drug on human participants:

     ▪ Phase I: Small-scale trials to assess safety, dosage, and side effects in a small group of healthy volunteers.

     ▪ Phase II: Larger trials to evaluate the drug's effectiveness and side effects in patients with the condition it aims to treat.

     ▪ Phase III: Large-scale trials to confirm the drug's effectiveness, monitor side effects, and compare it to existing treatments.

4. **Regulatory Approval**

   o Once a drug passes the clinical trial phases, the data is submitted to regulatory bodies such as the U.S. Food and Drug Administration (FDA) or the European Medicines Agency (EMA) for approval. Regulatory agencies thoroughly review the data to ensure the drug is safe and effective for public use. If approved, the drug is released to the market.

Time and Cost in Traditional Drug Development

The entire process of bringing a new drug to market is time-consuming and expensive. On average, it takes about **10 to 15 years** for a drug to progress from initial discovery to regulatory approval. This long timeline reflects the numerous stages involved, with each stage requiring significant resources, research, and testing. The **cost** of developing a new drug is also substantial, with estimates ranging from **$2 billion to $3 billion** or more. These high costs are driven by the need for extensive research, clinical trials, manufacturing, and regulatory compliance.

One of the primary reasons why drug development is so expensive is the high rate of **failure**. The pharmaceutical industry has one of the highest failure rates in any sector, with about **90% of drug candidates** that enter clinical trials failing to reach the market. This failure rate is particularly high in later-stage clinical trials, when drugs are tested on a larger group of patients and more variables come into play. Even drugs that show promise in early trials may fail during Phase III trials due to unforeseen safety concerns, side effects, or ineffectiveness.

The failure rate, combined with the enormous costs of conducting clinical trials, contributes to the overall financial burden of drug development. Companies that successfully bring a drug to market must often recoup the substantial costs of failed trials, making new drugs exceedingly expensive for patients.

The High Risks of Traditional Drug Development

Clinical Trial Failures

One of the greatest challenges in drug development is the uncertainty inherent in clinical trials. Despite preclinical testing and early-phase trials, there is always a significant degree of risk when it comes to human trials. Clinical trials are designed to test how a drug behaves in real-world conditions, and there are numerous factors that can influence whether a drug will succeed or fail. Some of the most common reasons why drugs fail in clinical trials include:

- **Ineffectiveness**: A drug that shows promise in early stages may fail to deliver the desired therapeutic effect in human patients. This is especially true for complex diseases such as cancer, Alzheimer's, and rare genetic disorders, where identifying an effective treatment is extraordinarily challenging.
- **Safety Concerns**: Even when a drug seems effective, unexpected side effects can emerge

45

during clinical trials. These side effects may be too severe or too common to justify the drug's approval. Many drugs are abandoned during Phase III trials due to safety concerns.

- **Inconsistent Results**: Drugs may perform well in early trials but fail to show consistent results in larger-scale trials. Variability in patient response, including genetic factors, can play a major role in a drug's success or failure.

- **Lack of Market Viability**: Sometimes drugs fail because they are not significantly better than existing treatments. In cases where there are already established therapies for a particular disease, a new drug must demonstrate clear advantages in terms of effectiveness, safety, and cost.

These uncertainties contribute to the **high financial risks** faced by pharmaceutical companies. For every drug that successfully reaches the market, many more fail, leaving companies to absorb the substantial costs of those unsuccessful trials. Furthermore, these failures can delay or prevent the approval of potentially life-saving treatments, impacting patients who rely on the availability of new medications.

Regulatory Hurdles

Another challenge in traditional drug development is the complexity of regulatory approval. Once clinical trials are completed, pharmaceutical companies must submit extensive data to regulatory agencies for review. These agencies, such as the FDA or EMA, require rigorous documentation of a drug's safety, efficacy, and quality. While these agencies serve to protect public health, the approval process can be lengthy, with drugs often taking years to receive regulatory clearance.

The regulatory process involves multiple stages, including:

- **Data Review**: Regulatory agencies review all data from preclinical studies, clinical trials, and manufacturing processes. This review can take several years, depending on the complexity of the drug and the disease it is intended to treat.
- **Inspection and Audits**: Agencies may conduct inspections of manufacturing facilities to ensure

that drugs are produced according to strict quality standards.

- **Labeling and Marketing Approval**: In addition to approving a drug's safety and efficacy, regulatory bodies also review its labeling and marketing materials. This step ensures that the drug's benefits and risks are clearly communicated to patients and healthcare providers.

The regulatory process is essential for ensuring that drugs are safe and effective, but it adds time and cost to the development process. Delays in approval can result in significant financial losses for pharmaceutical companies, particularly if a competitor manages to bring a similar drug to market first.

How AI Aims to Revolutionize Drug Development

The Promise of AI

Artificial intelligence is poised to address many of the challenges associated with traditional drug development. By leveraging machine learning algorithms, deep learning, and big data analytics, AI can significantly speed up the drug discovery process, reduce costs, and improve the accuracy of clinical trials. Let's explore how AI is making a difference in various stages of drug development.

1. **Accelerating Drug Discovery**

   o Traditionally, drug discovery involved high-throughput screening of thousands or even millions of compounds to identify potential candidates. This process is slow and expensive. AI, however, can analyze vast amounts of biological data and predict how different molecules will interact with specific targets in the body. Machine learning models can analyze genomic, proteomic, and chemical data to identify new drug candidates, vastly speeding up the discovery process. AI can also predict the toxicity, efficacy, and potential side effects of these compounds, reducing the need for time-consuming and costly laboratory experiments.

2. **Reducing Clinical Trial Failures**

- o AI can help reduce the high failure rate of clinical trials by improving patient selection and trial design. By analyzing patient data, including genetic profiles, medical histories, and previous treatments, AI can help identify patients who are most likely to benefit from a particular drug. This precision medicine approach increases the likelihood of success in clinical trials. AI can also be used to simulate clinical trials, predicting how different patient populations will respond to a treatment and optimizing trial designs accordingly.

3. **Streamlining Regulatory Approval**

- o AI can assist with regulatory approval by automating the review of clinical trial data, ensuring that all necessary information is included in submissions. Machine learning algorithms can also be used to analyze trends and predict potential issues in drug approval, allowing companies to address concerns before they arise. In some cases, AI can even help regulatory agencies identify patterns in safety data that may not be immediately obvious, aiding in faster decision-making.

4. **Optimizing   Drug   Manufacturing**

- o AI has the potential to optimize drug manufacturing processes by predicting and controlling variables that impact production quality. AI models can analyze data from production facilities to ensure that drugs are manufactured to the highest standards, reducing the risk of errors and inconsistencies.

The traditional drug development process is slow, costly, and fraught with risks. From the high rates of failure in clinical trials to the lengthy regulatory approval process, pharmaceutical companies face significant challenges in bringing new drugs to market. However, the rise of artificial intelligence offers a promising solution. AI can accelerate drug discovery, reduce the failure rate of clinical trials, streamline regulatory approval, and optimize manufacturing processes.

As AI technologies continue to evolve, the pharmaceutical industry is likely to experience profound changes. By embracing AI, companies can reduce the time and cost of developing new drugs, ultimately improving access to life-saving treatments. For patients, this means faster access to effective therapies and a greater likelihood of successful outcomes in clinical trials. The future of drug development may be defined by the powerful potential of AI, ushering in a new era of more efficient, cost-effective, and successful drug discovery.

Chapter 4: AI's Role in Target Identification and Drug Design

Artificial intelligence (AI) has emerged as a game-changing technology in the pharmaceutical industry, transforming the way researchers approach target identification and drug design. The traditional drug discovery process is often slow, costly, and fraught with inefficiencies. However, with AI-powered tools, researchers are making strides in overcoming these barriers, significantly speeding up the process of identifying potential disease targets and designing drugs that are more effective, precise, and safer. In this article, we will explore how AI is reshaping the identification of disease targets and the design of drugs to combat a range of conditions, from rare genetic disorders to complex diseases like cancer and Alzheimer's.

Understanding Target Identification and Drug Design

Before delving into the transformative role of AI, it is important to understand the two key components of the drug discovery process that AI is revolutionizing: target identification and drug design.

1. **Target Identification:**

   o **Target identification** refers to the process of identifying a molecular target—typically a gene, protein, or other biomolecule—that plays a crucial role in the development or progression of a disease. This target is then used as the focus of drug development, with the aim of designing compounds that can modulate its activity to treat the disease.

   o Traditionally, target identification involved studying diseases at a molecular level, using laboratory experiments, and leveraging biological databases to find potential targets. However, this process is time-consuming and may involve a great deal of trial and error.

o   With AI, the task of identifying disease targets has become more precise and efficient, enabling researchers to explore vast amounts of biological data and extract meaningful insights faster than ever before.

2. **Drug   Design:**

o   Once a target has been identified, researchers then design drugs that can interact with it in specific ways. This process, known as **drug design**, traditionally relied on high-throughput screening, where thousands of compounds are tested to identify those that bind to the target. This approach can be expensive, time-consuming, and inefficient.

o   AI has introduced a new paradigm for drug design, with **generative models** and other machine learning tools that allow researchers to predict and generate novel drug candidates. These AI algorithms can simulate how different molecules will interact with the target, optimizing the drug design process and increasing the likelihood of success in clinical trials.

AI in Target Identification

The process of identifying new disease targets has traditionally been one of the most challenging and resource-intensive aspects of drug discovery. AI, however, has changed the landscape by enabling faster and more accurate identification of potential targets.

1. Mining Big Data with Machine Learning

One of the key ways AI has enhanced target identification is by allowing researchers to mine vast amounts of biological data. In the past, scientists relied on experimental techniques, such as gene sequencing and protein assays, to identify potential disease targets. While these methods are valuable, they can be slow and often miss important patterns in the data. AI, particularly machine learning (ML), can analyze large datasets more efficiently and detect patterns that human researchers may not immediately see.

For example, machine learning algorithms can be trained on data from genomic, transcriptomic, and proteomic studies to identify correlations between specific genes, proteins, and diseases. These correlations can reveal new targets that could be modulated by drugs. Additionally, AI can help to **predict potential biomarkers** for diseases, which are measurable indicators that can be used to monitor disease progression or the effectiveness of a treatment.

Researchers have already begun to leverage machine learning models that use patient data to predict potential therapeutic targets for diseases such as cancer, Alzheimer's disease, and autoimmune disorders. By feeding data from various sources—such as electronic health records (EHRs), clinical trials, and patient genetic profiles—into AI systems, researchers can gain deeper insights into how diseases manifest at the molecular level and identify potential targets for drug intervention.

2. AI-Driven Drug Repurposing

Another application of AI in target identification is in **drug repurposing**, where existing drugs are tested against new diseases or targets. AI systems can analyze existing drug databases and predict how well a particular drug might interact with different molecular targets. For example, an AI model might identify an existing cancer drug that could also be effective against a different type of cancer or a neurological disorder.

AI-driven drug repurposing has already led to successful discoveries. For example, AI was used to identify **baricitinib**, an existing drug for rheumatoid arthritis, as a potential treatment for COVID-19. This type of rapid, data-driven drug repurposing could significantly reduce the time and cost of developing new treatments, especially in situations where urgent medical needs arise, such as pandemics or rare diseases.

3. AI and Multi-Omic Data Integration

Disease processes often involve the interplay of multiple biological systems, including genes, proteins, metabolites, and environmental factors. These interactions can be difficult to study using traditional methods. However, AI enables the integration of various **multi-omic datasets** (such as genomics, proteomics, metabolomics, and epigenomics), providing a more comprehensive understanding of the underlying biology of diseases.

AI systems can be trained to integrate these diverse data types, revealing intricate biological pathways and identifying key nodes that could serve as disease targets. For example, AI tools can identify not only individual proteins or genes involved in a disease but also the relationships between these molecules and how they contribute to the disease's progression.

This integrative approach can reveal new, **less obvious** disease targets that may not have been considered through conventional methods, helping researchers discover novel therapeutic strategies and drug candidates.

AI in Drug Design

Once a target has been identified, the next step is to design drugs that can modulate its activity. AI is significantly improving this phase of drug discovery by enhancing the design, optimization, and testing of potential drug candidates.

1. Generative Models for Drug Design

AI, particularly generative models, is transforming drug design by automating the creation of novel molecules. Generative models, such as **Generative Adversarial Networks (GANs)** and **variational autoencoders (VAEs)**, can generate new drug-like molecules that bind to the target of interest. These models learn from large datasets of known drug structures and use this knowledge to propose new compounds that are likely to have the desired properties.

For example, **Insilico Medicine**, a company at the forefront of AI-driven drug discovery, uses generative AI to design novel molecules that target specific proteins involved in diseases such as cancer, fibrosis, and Alzheimer's disease. These AI models can quickly propose thousands of potential drug candidates, significantly reducing the time required for hit identification and optimization.

By using AI to **predict molecular interactions**, researchers can design molecules that fit the shape and chemical properties of the target protein, improving the likelihood of successful binding and therapeutic efficacy. Moreover, AI can optimize these molecules for properties such as **solubility, stability**, and **bioavailability**, which are critical for drug development.

2. Predicting Drug-Target Interactions

AI algorithms are highly effective at predicting how small molecules will interact with their targets. Machine learning models, including **deep learning** approaches, can be trained on large databases of known drug-target interactions to predict how new compounds will bind to specific proteins. These predictions allow researchers to identify promising drug candidates before they are tested in the lab, which can save time and reduce the need for high-throughput screening.

Deep learning models such as **convolutional neural networks (CNNs)** and **recurrent neural networks (RNNs)** are particularly adept at recognizing patterns in complex datasets, such as protein structures and molecular fingerprints. For example, deep learning models can be used to predict how a compound will interact with a protein's binding site based on the compound's chemical structure. This helps researchers design drugs that are more likely to be effective and reduces the chances of failures in preclinical testing.

3. Drug Toxicity and Side Effects Prediction

A major challenge in drug design is predicting and mitigating the potential **toxicity** and **side effects** of new compounds. Adverse reactions are one of the leading causes of drug failures during clinical trials. AI models can assist in predicting toxicity by analyzing chemical structures and historical data on known drug side effects.

AI tools can be trained to recognize molecular features associated with toxicity and side effects, allowing researchers to filter out compounds that are likely to cause harm before they enter clinical trials. For example, AI systems can analyze patterns in large chemical datasets to predict how a drug might affect organs such as the liver or kidneys, or whether it might have carcinogenic properties.

4. Virtual Screening and Optimization

AI can also accelerate the **virtual screening** process, which involves simulating how thousands of compounds will interact with a target. Traditionally, virtual screening was a labor-intensive process that required researchers to manually test compounds against a target protein. With AI, researchers can use machine learning models to automatically screen vast libraries of molecules and predict which ones are most likely to bind to the target.

Once promising compounds are identified, AI can further **optimize** these molecules by making adjustments to their chemical structure to improve efficacy, reduce toxicity, or enhance other properties. This iterative design process, powered by AI, allows researchers to refine drug candidates more efficiently, increasing the chances of success in clinical trials.

AI is fundamentally reshaping the fields of target identification and drug design, enabling pharmaceutical researchers to identify new disease targets and design effective drug candidates faster, cheaper, and more efficiently than ever before. Through advanced machine learning algorithms, AI is able to mine vast datasets, predict how molecules will interact with targets, and design novel compounds with higher accuracy. These advancements promise to accelerate the development of new treatments for a wide range of diseases, from cancers to rare genetic disorders.

As AI continues to evolve, the potential for more precise, personalized medicines increases. AI's ability to integrate data across multiple biological levels and simulate complex molecular interactions could lead to drug candidates that are not only more effective but also safer and more tailored to individual patients' needs. The combination of AI-driven target identification and drug design is paving the way for a new era in medicine, where faster and more accurate drug discovery could help address some of the world's most pressing health challenges.

Chapter 5: The Milestones and Successes of AI-Discovered Molecules

The pharmaceutical industry has long been burdened with the complexities of drug discovery. The process of bringing a new drug from the lab to market is fraught with challenges, including time-consuming research, astronomical costs, and a high failure rate. However, recent advancements in artificial intelligence (AI) have ushered in a new era in drug discovery, where AI-driven molecules are beginning to make their mark in clinical trials. These AI-discovered molecules represent a promising shift in how medicines are designed, offering the potential to significantly reduce the time and costs involved in developing effective treatments.

In this article, we explore the milestones and successes of AI-discovered molecules, examining the growing number of these molecules entering clinical trials. We will also delve into insights from experts in the field, shedding light on how AI is reshaping drug discovery and how its application in identifying new molecules could revolutionize the treatment of diseases across the globe.

The Role of AI in Drug Discovery

Drug discovery traditionally involves a lengthy process of screening large libraries of compounds to find those that interact with a biological target—often a protein, gene, or receptor—associated with a disease. Once a promising candidate is identified, it goes through several rounds of testing to determine its safety and efficacy, followed by clinical trials. This process takes, on average, 10 to 15 years and costs billions of dollars, with many drugs failing during clinical trials.

Artificial intelligence, however, has introduced a new approach. AI systems are particularly adept at analyzing large datasets, identifying patterns, and predicting which molecules are likely to interact with disease targets. AI's ability to sift through vast amounts of biological, chemical, and genetic data has accelerated the drug discovery process, enabling researchers to quickly identify potential drug candidates that might otherwise go unnoticed.

Moreover, AI systems can design new molecules with precision, significantly improving the chances of developing effective treatments.

As a result, the number of AI-discovered molecules entering clinical trials has been steadily increasing, and the success stories are beginning to accumulate.

Milestone 1: Insilico Medicine's Groundbreaking Achievements

One of the most prominent examples of AI-driven drug discovery is **Insilico Medicine**, a company founded in 2014 by Dr. Alex Zhavoronkov. Insilico Medicine uses artificial intelligence and machine learning algorithms to discover novel molecules for diseases that have proven difficult to treat. The company's approach focuses on applying AI across every stage of drug discovery, from identifying disease targets to designing drug molecules.

In 2020, Insilico Medicine made headlines when it became the first company to take an AI-discovered drug molecule into clinical trials. The drug, designed for the treatment of idiopathic pulmonary fibrosis (IPF)—a rare and progressive lung disease—was developed using

generative adversarial networks (GANs), a type of deep learning model that can create new molecular structures by learning from existing data. This marked a significant milestone in the AI-driven drug discovery field, as it demonstrated the potential of AI to not only identify drug targets but also to design drug candidates that are capable of undergoing clinical testing.

Dr. Zhavoronkov, the CEO of Insilico Medicine, explains, "Our machine learning algorithms are designed to optimize molecules, predicting which will bind to the target of interest and how they will behave in the human body. In this case, our AI system produced a molecule that fit all the criteria for treating IPF, including efficacy, safety, and bioavailability."

Following the success of this initial clinical trial, Insilico Medicine has continued to push the boundaries of AI in drug discovery. The company now has six molecules in clinical trials, with several others showing promising early-stage results. These molecules cover a wide range of diseases, including cancer, aging, and fibrosis, demonstrating the versatility of AI in tackling complex diseases.

Milestone 2: Alphabet's Isomorphic Labs and AI-Driven Drug Discovery

Another key player in AI-driven drug discovery is **Isomorphic Labs**, a company launched by Alphabet—the parent company of Google—in late 2021. Isomorphic Labs leverages Google's vast computational power and AI expertise to accelerate the drug discovery process. The company's mission is to apply AI models to drug design, using the same AI principles that have revolutionized other industries, such as natural language processing and image recognition.

Isomorphic Labs' AI-driven platform focuses on designing molecules to interact with specific biological targets, just as Google's AI models have been used to design algorithms for other domains. At the core of the company's approach is **DeepMind's AlphaFold**, an AI system that predicts the 3D structure of proteins with unprecedented accuracy. This breakthrough, which earned DeepMind a Nobel Prize in Chemistry in 2022, is a game-changer for drug discovery because it allows researchers to understand protein structures in detail, enabling them to design drugs that can more effectively target disease-related proteins.

The first AI-discovered molecule from Isomorphic Labs is currently undergoing testing, marking another milestone in the growing list of AI-driven drugs entering clinical trials. In the coming years, Isomorphic Labs hopes to push the boundaries of AI drug discovery, using its technology to find new treatments for a wide variety of diseases, including rare genetic disorders and conditions with unmet medical needs.

Milestone 3: AI-Discovered Molecules in Clinical Trials

As of 2023, the number of AI-discovered molecules entering clinical trials has been steadily increasing. According to a recent analysis by **Boston Consulting Group (BCG)**, at least 75 AI-discovered molecules have entered clinical trials, with many more expected in the coming years. This trend marks a significant shift in the drug discovery landscape, where AI is no longer seen as a niche technology but as a mainstream tool for accelerating drug development.

These AI-discovered molecules represent a wide variety of diseases, including cancer, autoimmune disorders, neurological diseases, and rare genetic conditions. For example, **Recursion Pharmaceuticals**, a company that uses AI to identify disease targets and design drugs, has developed a molecule for the treatment of both lymphoma and solid tumors. The molecule, discovered using AI models trained on large datasets of molecular and biological data, is currently undergoing early-phase clinical trials.

Similarly, **Atomwise**, a company that uses AI for drug discovery, has developed a promising AI-discovered molecule for the treatment of Ebola and other viral diseases. Atomwise's AI platform uses deep learning to predict how small molecules will interact with specific disease targets, speeding up the drug discovery process. The company's work has already led to several collaborations with pharmaceutical companies and research institutions, with its AI-discovered molecules being tested for a variety of diseases.

The fact that AI-discovered molecules are now routinely entering clinical trials is a testament to the growing confidence in AI's ability to identify and design drug candidates that are effective and safe for humans. Experts believe that this success will continue to build momentum, leading to more AI-discovered drugs entering the market in the future.

Successes of AI-Discovered Molecules: Insights from Experts

As AI-driven drug discovery continues to mature, many experts in the field have shared their insights on the transformative potential of AI in improving patient outcomes. According to **Chris Meier**, a partner at Boston Consulting Group, "The real breakthrough we are seeing is that AI is no longer just a tool for drug discovery, but a tool for transforming the entire drug development process." Meier notes that AI can reduce the time required to bring drugs to market, minimize costly failures, and increase the success rate of clinical trials.

Charlotte Deane, a professor of structural bioinformatics at Oxford University, also highlights the promise of AI in drug discovery. "We are at the beginning of a revolution," she says. "The combination of AI's ability to process vast amounts of data and human expertise in biology and chemistry will lead to a new era of drug discovery. It will allow us to tackle diseases that were once thought impossible to treat."

Dr. **Alex Zhavoronkov**, the founder of Insilico Medicine, further elaborates on the success of AI-discovered molecules: "What we are seeing now is the culmination of years of research and development in the field of AI. The molecules we have designed using AI are entering clinical trials with a high probability of success, which is a huge milestone for the pharmaceutical industry. This is just the beginning, and we expect to see many more successful AI-driven drug candidates in the years to come."

The Future of AI in Drug Discovery

The success of AI-discovered molecules entering clinical trials is only the beginning of what could be a revolution in drug development. As AI algorithms continue to improve and more data becomes available, the scope of AI-driven drug discovery will only expand. In the future, AI could play an even more prominent role in designing personalized medicines, where treatments are tailored to individual patients' genetic profiles.

Moreover, AI has the potential to dramatically reduce the cost and time required for clinical trials. Traditional clinical trials are expensive, time-consuming, and prone to high failure rates. AI can help optimize clinical trial design by predicting which patients are most likely to benefit from a treatment, improving patient recruitment, and identifying potential biomarkers that can be used to monitor the effectiveness of a drug.

As AI continues to evolve, it is expected that the number of AI-discovered molecules entering clinical trials will continue to rise, paving the way for more effective treatments for a range of diseases. With major players like Insilico Medicine, Isomorphic Labs, and Recursion Pharmaceuticals leading the charge, the future of drug discovery looks brighter than ever.

The increasing number of AI-discovered molecules entering clinical trials marks a turning point in the pharmaceutical industry. These milestones represent the growing success of AI in transforming drug discovery, enabling the identification of novel targets and the design of more effective, safer drugs. As the technology continues to mature, AI is set to revolutionize how we develop treatments for some of the world's most challenging diseases.

With the support of AI-driven companies like Insilico Medicine and Isomorphic Labs, the drug discovery process is becoming faster, more efficient, and less costly, offering hope for patients worldwide. The future of drug discovery is increasingly digital, and AI's role in identifying and designing new molecules is central to shaping the future of medicine.

Chapter 6: Challenges: Data Limitations and Biases in AI Drug Discovery

Artificial intelligence (AI) has emerged as a powerful tool in revolutionizing drug discovery, promising to accelerate the identification of new treatments, reduce development costs, and streamline clinical trial processes. With the potential to analyze vast amounts of biological, chemical, and genetic data, AI models have already begun to reshape how pharmaceutical companies approach drug development. However, as with any transformative technology, the adoption of AI in drug discovery is not without its challenges. Two of the most significant obstacles in AI-driven drug discovery are data limitations and biases, which can hinder the ability of AI systems to make accurate predictions and lead to suboptimal results.

This article explores the challenges of data scarcity and biases in AI drug discovery, highlighting the hurdles that AI faces in analyzing medical and biological data. We will also examine how companies like **Recursion Pharmaceuticals** are addressing these challenges, striving to create solutions that allow AI to fulfill its promise in the drug development process.

The Role of Data in AI-Driven Drug Discovery

AI models, particularly machine learning algorithms, rely heavily on large datasets to identify patterns and make predictions. In drug discovery, these models are trained on a variety of biological, chemical, and clinical data, such as the molecular structures of compounds, biological pathways, protein structures, genetic data, and clinical trial outcomes. The more data that an AI model is exposed to, the better it becomes at making predictions about the effectiveness of a given drug candidate. Ideally, AI systems can analyze these datasets to predict how different molecules will interact with disease-related proteins, allowing researchers to identify promising drug candidates with higher accuracy than traditional methods.

However, for AI to function optimally in drug discovery, the data it works with must be abundant, high-quality, and diverse. Unfortunately, the reality is that data in the pharmaceutical industry is often scarce, fragmented, or incomplete, posing significant challenges for AI models. Moreover, even when data is available, it may be subject to biases that can distort the outcomes of AI predictions, leading to erroneous conclusions that could slow the development of effective drugs.

Data Scarcity in Drug Discovery

One of the main limitations that AI faces in drug discovery is the scarcity of high-quality, well-curated data. The pharmaceutical industry has made significant strides in generating large datasets, particularly with advancements in genomic sequencing and high-throughput screening technologies. However, despite these advancements, high-quality, comprehensive datasets are still relatively rare in many therapeutic areas, especially for rare diseases, genetic disorders, and complex conditions like cancer and neurological diseases.

For example, rare diseases often lack extensive patient data due to their low prevalence, making it difficult for AI models to find enough examples to identify relevant patterns. This scarcity of data creates a situation where AI models are either trained on limited information or on datasets that do not fully represent the diversity of biological systems. As a result, AI models may struggle to make accurate predictions, which could delay the discovery of effective treatments.

In oncology, for instance, while there is a large amount of genomic and clinical data for certain types of cancer, less common cancers do not have the same wealth of data available. AI models may find it difficult to predict how potential drug candidates will perform against these rarer types of cancer if they are not exposed to sufficient data during the training phase.

Furthermore, clinical trial data, which is essential for evaluating the efficacy and safety of potential drug candidates, is often limited by the structure of the trials themselves. Clinical trials are usually conducted on specific patient populations under highly controlled conditions, and the resulting datasets may not reflect the broader population of patients who will eventually use the drug in the real world. This lack of diversity in clinical data poses a significant challenge for AI models attempting to predict the effectiveness of drugs in diverse patient populations.

Addressing Data Scarcity: Recursion Pharmaceuticals

One company tackling the issue of data scarcity head-on is **Recursion Pharmaceuticals**. Recursion uses AI and machine learning algorithms to explore biological and chemical data to identify novel drug candidates. The company's approach is particularly focused on overcoming the challenge of limited data by generating vast amounts of data through **automated experimental platforms**.

Recursion's technology platform combines high-content screening with AI to generate massive quantities of data related to the human biology of disease. By applying machine learning algorithms to analyze the resulting data, Recursion can make predictions about how different compounds might interact with disease targets. This approach allows Recursion to create large datasets that can help address data scarcity, even for conditions with limited available information.

Recursion's strategy of generating experimental data to supplement existing datasets has already led to the discovery of promising drug candidates for several diseases, including cancer and rare genetic disorders. By building and maintaining large-scale, comprehensive datasets, Recursion is helping to ensure that its AI models are trained on high-quality, diverse data, which enhances the accuracy and relevance of its predictions.

This data-centric approach allows Recursion to tackle complex diseases for which traditional data may be lacking, giving AI the information it needs to make informed predictions about potential drug efficacy.

Biases in AI Drug Discovery

In addition to data scarcity, **biases in data** pose another significant challenge to AI in drug discovery. Biases can arise in many ways, including from unrepresentative datasets, faulty data collection practices, or inherent biases in clinical trials. These biases can be particularly problematic when it comes to healthcare, as they can lead to AI systems making inaccurate predictions that disproportionately affect certain groups of patients.

For example, if the data used to train an AI model for drug discovery predominantly comes from one demographic group—say, Caucasian males—the AI may develop a bias that makes it less effective at predicting drug responses in other populations, such as women or people from different racial or ethnic backgrounds. This can result in drug candidates that are less effective or safe for underrepresented populations, exacerbating health disparities and limiting the overall success of AI-driven drug discovery.

AI models can also be biased based on the types of diseases represented in the data. If the data used to train an AI system primarily comes from certain therapeutic areas, such as oncology, it may not generalize well to other disease areas, such as rare diseases or neurological conditions. This could lead to AI-driven discoveries that are biased toward the diseases for which data is more readily available, rather than addressing the full spectrum of medical needs.

Additionally, biases can be introduced by the methods used to collect and analyze clinical trial data. For example, clinical trials often include limited patient demographics, which may skew the data and create a false impression of a drug's efficacy or safety profile across a broader population.

Tackling Biases: Recursion Pharmaceuticals' Approach

Recursion Pharmaceuticals is addressing the issue of biases through its commitment to building diverse, comprehensive datasets that can help eliminate some of the biases that can emerge during the drug discovery process. The company's AI platform generates data from a wide range of biological contexts, incorporating various cell lines, disease models, and patient-derived samples. This diverse data is used to train AI models, helping to minimize biases that may arise from more narrowly defined datasets.

In addition, Recursion's machine learning algorithms are designed to detect and address biases in the data by considering variables like age, sex, and genetic background when making predictions about drug efficacy. By incorporating these factors into its models, Recursion aims to create more equitable drug discovery processes that produce better outcomes for diverse patient populations.

Moreover, Recursion's emphasis on generating large-scale data through high-content screening allows the company to address biases that may arise from limited clinical trial data. By supplementing clinical trial data with a wider range of experimental data, Recursion is able to reduce the potential for biases that could impact the development of new drugs.

The Importance of Data Sharing and Collaboration

Overcoming the challenges of data scarcity and biases in AI-driven drug discovery will require widespread collaboration and data sharing across the pharmaceutical and biotech industries. One of the key barriers to data sharing is the proprietary nature of many datasets, particularly clinical trial data. Pharmaceutical companies often guard their clinical data closely, as it can be a valuable asset in the race to develop new drugs.

However, some companies, including Recursion Pharmaceuticals, are taking a more open approach to data sharing. Recursion has partnered with several academic institutions and research organizations to share data and collaborate on drug discovery projects. By pooling resources and knowledge, these collaborations aim to accelerate the development of new treatments and ensure that AI models are trained on diverse, representative datasets.

In addition to collaboration between companies, public-private partnerships are also emerging to address data scarcity and biases. For instance, the **Global Alliance for Genomics and Health (GA4GH)** is a coalition of organizations dedicated to improving the sharing and accessibility of genomic data. Such initiatives are helping to bridge gaps in the data available for AI-driven drug discovery, making it easier for AI systems to analyze diverse, high-quality datasets.

AI has the potential to revolutionize drug discovery by reducing development times, costs, and the number of failures in clinical trials. However, for AI to reach its full potential, it must overcome significant challenges related to data scarcity and biases. Companies like Recursion Pharmaceuticals are at the forefront of tackling these challenges by generating large-scale, diverse datasets and developing AI models that account for potential biases.

As AI continues to evolve in the drug discovery space, addressing these data-related challenges will be critical for ensuring that AI models are accurate, equitable, and capable of making impactful predictions. By fostering collaboration and data sharing across the industry, AI-driven drug discovery can reach new heights, ultimately improving outcomes for patients and creating new treatments for diseases that have long remained untreatable.

Chapter 7: The Future of AI in Medicine: Hopes and Uncertainties

The use of Artificial Intelligence (AI) in medicine is one of the most promising frontiers in modern healthcare, with the potential to revolutionize areas such as drug discovery, personalized treatment, diagnostics, and patient care. Over the last few years, AI has increasingly become integrated into medical practices, offering capabilities far beyond traditional methods. From speeding up drug discovery processes to predicting patient outcomes with more precision, AI's applications in healthcare are profound. However, despite the excitement and progress, there are still significant uncertainties surrounding the technology's role in medicine. As the adoption of AI in healthcare accelerates, experts in the field continue to evaluate its potential and recognize the hurdles it must overcome.

This article will explore both the hopes and uncertainties surrounding AI's future in medicine, particularly in drug discovery, highlighting the voices of experts and discussing the importance of clinical trial validation, regulatory considerations, and ongoing efforts to ensure the safe and ethical use of AI in healthcare.

The Promising Potential of AI in Medicine

Revolutionizing Drug Discovery

One of the most well-discussed applications of AI in medicine is its impact on drug discovery. The traditional drug development process has long been known for its inefficiency and high costs. It is a time-consuming and costly endeavor that often takes 10 to 15 years and upwards of $2 billion to bring a new drug to market. A staggering 90% of drugs that enter clinical trials ultimately fail, representing a significant waste of time, money, and resources. This high failure rate has fueled the search for alternative, more efficient methods for drug discovery.

AI has the potential to transform this process by improving how we discover new drug candidates. By analyzing vast amounts of biological data, AI models can help identify potential therapeutic targets, design molecules, and predict the success of drug candidates before they reach clinical trials. Moreover, AI can optimize clinical trial designs, monitor patient outcomes, and ensure that drugs are safe and effective. Early-stage AI models, like those used by companies such as **Insilico Medicine** and **Recursion Pharmaceuticals**, are already helping identify novel drug candidates, some of which have progressed to clinical trials.

Dr. **Alex Zhavoronkov**, the CEO of Insilico Medicine, is one of the leading voices in the AI-driven drug discovery space. According to him, AI can dramatically speed up the drug discovery process, which traditionally involved testing thousands of compounds manually in laboratories. AI systems can quickly generate and analyze molecular designs, assess their potential efficacy, and predict how they might interact with the human body. In doing so, AI significantly reduces the need for labor-intensive testing and enhances the likelihood of success in later-stage clinical trials.

For example, Insilico Medicine has already used AI to discover molecules that are being tested in clinical trials for diseases such as idiopathic pulmonary fibrosis (IPF), a rare and fatal lung disease. AI also played a crucial role in identifying a promising treatment for cancer and other conditions.

Enhancing Precision Medicine

In addition to drug discovery, AI is contributing to the growing field of **precision medicine**, which tailors medical treatment to individual patients based on their genetic makeup, lifestyle, and environmental factors. Precision medicine holds the promise of providing more effective treatments while minimizing adverse side effects by taking into account a patient's unique genetic profile.

AI plays a crucial role in analyzing genetic and clinical data to match patients with the most appropriate treatments. For example, AI algorithms are being used to predict how patients will respond to specific cancer therapies based on the genetic alterations present in their tumors. **IBM Watson Health**, one of the leaders in the AI healthcare space, has been using its AI platform to analyze unstructured medical data (such as doctors' notes, patient histories, and genetic information) to help oncologists recommend personalized treatment options.

Furthermore, AI can help detect diseases early by recognizing patterns in medical images, such as X-rays, MRIs, and CT scans, that may be too subtle for human doctors to identify. Early detection has long been a cornerstone of improving patient outcomes, and AI can enhance this process by automating image analysis, leading to faster diagnoses and more timely interventions.

Improving Diagnostics and Patient Outcomes

Beyond drug discovery and precision medicine, AI holds enormous promise in improving diagnostics and patient outcomes. Machine learning algorithms are increasingly being used in radiology, dermatology, cardiology, and pathology to analyze medical images, pathology slides, and other forms of data to help clinicians make more accurate diagnoses. **Deep learning** models, a subset of machine learning, have demonstrated exceptional performance in diagnosing conditions such as breast cancer, skin cancer, and eye diseases with accuracy that rivals or even exceeds that of human doctors.

AI can also be used to predict patient outcomes by analyzing data from electronic health records (EHRs). For example, AI models can predict which patients are at high risk of developing complications after surgery or which patients might experience a relapse of cancer. This enables healthcare providers to make more informed decisions, prioritize high-risk patients, and personalize treatment plans.

Experts such as **Dr. Eric Topol**, a cardiologist and prominent advocate for AI in medicine, argue that AI can significantly improve the way doctors deliver care. He believes AI has the potential to complement the work of healthcare professionals, allowing them to focus on more complex aspects of patient care while automating routine tasks such as data analysis and image interpretation.

Uncertainties and Challenges

Despite the promising future of AI in medicine, there are significant uncertainties and challenges that need to be addressed. Experts agree that, although AI has great potential, it is not a "silver bullet" that will instantly solve all the problems in drug discovery or patient care. Some of the major concerns include:

The Need for Clinical Trial Validation

One of the most pressing challenges surrounding AI in medicine is the **need for clinical validation**. While AI models can provide promising predictions based on historical data, they must be rigorously tested in real-world clinical trials to prove their efficacy and safety. Clinical trials remain the gold standard for validating any new treatment or drug, and the same should apply to AI-based discoveries.

Even if AI systems predict promising drug candidates or diagnostic tools, these predictions must be verified through extensive clinical trials. AI may help streamline the design of these trials, but the actual testing of drug efficacy in patients is an indispensable part of the process. For example, many AI-driven drug discoveries have progressed to clinical trials, but it is still uncertain whether these drugs will achieve the same level of success as predicted by the AI models. **Regulatory bodies like the FDA** require evidence from well-conducted clinical trials before they approve any new drugs for the market, and the failure rate of drugs in clinical trials remains high.

Moreover, AI models often rely on historical data, which may not always account for new, emerging trends or unforeseen variables. **Dr. David J. Fajgenbaum**, a researcher focused on AI in medicine, notes that while AI can predict a drug's potential success in clinical trials, it cannot fully anticipate the complexities and nuances of human biology and the myriad factors that may affect the outcome of a trial.

Ethical and Regulatory Concerns

The ethical implications of using AI in medicine are another area of uncertainty. AI models can be vulnerable to biases based on the data they are trained on, and these biases could have serious consequences in healthcare. For example, if AI algorithms are trained predominantly on data from one demographic group, the results may be skewed and less accurate for other populations. This is particularly concerning in areas like drug discovery, where AI might produce biased predictions that could harm marginalized communities or exclude certain populations from access to new treatments.

Furthermore, AI raises significant **regulatory challenges**. Current healthcare regulations are designed for traditional medical research and drug discovery, not for AI-driven processes. Regulatory bodies like the U.S. FDA and the European Medicines Agency (EMA) are working to develop new frameworks for evaluating AI-based medical devices and drugs, but these regulations are still in their infancy. The lack of standardized guidelines for AI applications in healthcare means that companies may struggle to bring AI-driven products to market quickly and efficiently.

In addition, as AI technology continues to evolve, there are concerns about **data privacy and security**. AI models often require access to sensitive patient data, and there is an ongoing need to ensure that this data is protected from misuse or cyberattacks. Data privacy laws like the **Health Insurance Portability and Accountability Act (HIPAA)** in the U.S. have been designed to protect patient confidentiality, but AI raises questions about how such regulations can keep pace with technological advancements.

The Role of Human Expertise

AI is undoubtedly powerful, but its role in medicine is ultimately complementary to human expertise. Experts agree that AI should not replace doctors but rather serve as a tool that enhances their decision-making abilities. While AI can analyze data and make predictions, it cannot replace the nuanced understanding that human doctors have of patient care, ethics, and communication. In drug discovery, AI can generate and test hypotheses, but scientists still need to interpret the results and make decisions about which compounds to pursue further.

Dr. Charlotte Deane, a professor at the University of Oxford specializing in structural bioinformatics, stresses that AI will work best when used in conjunction with human judgment. She believes that scientists and clinicians will need to work alongside AI systems, using their expertise to guide AI-based decisions and ensure that the technology is used in ethically sound ways.

AI's future in medicine is filled with promise, yet it is not without uncertainties. On one hand, AI has the potential to revolutionize drug discovery, diagnostics, personalized treatment, and patient care by improving efficiency, accuracy, and outcomes. The speed at which AI can analyze vast datasets holds great promise for accelerating drug development, while AI's ability to offer personalized treatment recommendations could reshape how doctors approach patient care.

On the other hand, the technology faces significant challenges, including the need for clinical validation, regulatory hurdles, biases in AI models, and ethical considerations. The role of human expertise will remain critical in ensuring that AI tools are used appropriately and responsibly.

Experts agree that while AI has the potential to transform healthcare, ongoing research, clinical trials, and regulatory efforts are essential to harness its full potential safely and ethically. As AI technology continues to evolve, it will require collaboration between researchers, clinicians, regulatory bodies, and policymakers to navigate the complexities of its integration into medicine. Only through careful validation and responsible use can AI live up to its transformative potential in healthcare.

Conclusion

The integration of Artificial Intelligence (AI) into medicine represents one of the most profound transformations in the history of healthcare. As explored throughout this book, AI's potential to revolutionize drug discovery, diagnostics, treatment personalization, and patient care is immense. By leveraging the power of AI, researchers and clinicians are accelerating the discovery of new treatments, improving the precision of diagnoses, and enhancing patient outcomes. From companies like Insilico Medicine and Isomorphic Labs to groundbreaking innovations in personalized medicine, the contributions of AI are reshaping how we understand and address complex diseases.

However, this exciting new frontier is not without its challenges. The process of integrating AI into medicine must navigate hurdles such as data limitations, biases in algorithms, regulatory issues, and the critical need for robust clinical validation. As AI tools continue to evolve, they must be rigorously tested in clinical settings to ensure they live up to their potential and, importantly, do so without compromising patient safety or ethical standards. The role of human expertise remains indispensable in guiding AI's application, ensuring that it is used to complement the work of clinicians rather than replace it.

Looking ahead, the future of AI in medicine holds great promise but requires thoughtful, responsible adoption. We stand at the cusp of a new era where AI has the potential to reduce the time and cost of drug development, revolutionize disease treatment, and provide more tailored, effective care for patients. However, to fully realize this vision, there must be continued collaboration between AI technologists, healthcare professionals, and regulators. Only through collective efforts and careful oversight can AI's transformative power be harnessed to improve the healthcare landscape for all.

In conclusion, while we are only beginning to understand the full potential of AI in medicine, the progress made so far suggests that we are on the precipice of a new age in healthcare. The hopes for better, faster, and more effective treatments are within reach, but the path forward will require careful attention to both technological advancement and ethical considerations. With the right strategies, AI could indeed redefine the future of medicine, making healthcare more efficient, personalized, and accessible for people around the world.

www.ingramcontent.com/pod-product-compliance
Lightning Source LLC
LaVergne TN
LVHW051714050326
832903LV00032B/4192